365

Felicia Guy-Lynch

To: Clarence

From: Julina

7/13/13

Thanks for the support !! :)

Enjoy ♥

ISBN 978-1481868679

www.feliciaguylynch.com

dedication

Kristopher Robinson thanks for the idea that sparked the manifestation of the book

Bradley Lindsay thank you for gently reminding me of the simple things: they will go a long way

One day at a time…

January 1st

Kill them with kindness

Control the day or it controls you

January 3rd

You only fail when you quit

Be around those who only uplift

January 5th

Be now what you foresee to come

Like wine, age and grow sweeter

January 7th

Go ham or get fried up

January 8th

Be your own biggest motivator

January 9th

Keep balanced when it gets steep

Grow as you go through life

January 11th

Prepare for the least, hope for the best

Take the world by storm gently

January 13th

Best things in life are priceless

Deeds speak words whisper

Lay a foundation with bricks thrown at you

Make life an offer it can't refuse

January 17th

Go ahead, make your day

January 18th

May the Most High be with you

January 19th

Don't just run the field, make sure you score

Truth offends but sets us free

January 21st

Practice at home before you practice abroad

Be the headstone the builder refused

January 23th

Learning is a journey, not a destination

Immunity to criticism keeps you healthy

Be strongest in defenselessness

Action with vision is for dreamers

January 27th

Sing in the life boat during a shipwreck

What we dwell on is who we'll be

January 29th

Defeat is bitter when tasted and swallowed

See a stumbling block as a stepping stone

January 31st

The cup is half full for the optimist

Strive to only be you

February 2nd

Let your faith carry you through hard times

Don't stress what you can't control

February 4th

Speak the truth or don't speak at all

February 5th

Nothing happens before its time

February 6th

Seek wisdom while you gather knowledge

Track your life by smiles not sorrow

February 8th

Simplest things are the most extraordinary

Be content: it could have been worse

February 10th

Knowledge articulates, wisdom observes

There's what you plan for life vs. what life has planned for you

February 12th

Nice to know, better to innerstand

Love limitlessly

February 14th

Risking nothing is the greatest hazard

Make more opportunities than you find

February 16th

Wisdom is learning how to think

February 17th

Your treasure lies in what you offer

Know what to overlook

Kill time without hurting immortality

February 20th

Take your time you'll stumble when you rush

Take what you do seriously not yourself

February 22nd

Don't give up, you're too close

February 23rd

Almost doesn't count: complete it

February 24th

See yourself in others: you'll never judge again

Build a door if opportunity has yet to knock

February 26th

Listen twice as much as you speak

Face your fears: you'll feel encouraged

February 28th

Without consent, you can't feel inferior

Create your own positive affirmation

March 1st

Hire courage, fire insecurity

A good speaker tugs the hearts of their listeners

March 3rd

Drunken man's words are a sober man's thoughts

March 4th

Realize how light you become when you rid your burdens

March 5th

Breathe

Keep your dreams alive

March 7th

Health is wealth

Happiness doesn't decrease when shared

Fear not what you'll become

Be subtle to the point of abstraction

Be mysterious to the point of quietness

March 12th

Evolve

March 13th

Know thyself

Break resistance without fighting

March 15th

All or nothing

To each his or her own

March 17th

They can't ride your back unless it's bent

Integrity ends when you're silent about what matters

March 19th

Have infinite hope in the midst of finite disappointment

Build dams of bravery to block floods of doubt

March 21st

A kind response turns away wrath

Quality over quantity

March 23rd

Persist what you resist

March 24th

I am

March 25th

Get busy doing nothing once in a while

Agree to disagree

March 27th

Observe your surroundings

Time is of the essence

March 29th

Healing starts within

True freedom comes with the freedom to make mistakes

March 31st

There's much strength in forgiveness

April 1st

Jokes on you

April 2ⁿᵈ

Complacency leads to stagnation

Everything is everything

April 4th

You are never really alone

If you don't start building your own dream, you help build another

If you don't ask, you won't know

You can't lose what you never gained

April 8th

Words can't be killed

Learn from your past

Musical expression is important for progression

Know when to leave, don't over stay you presence

April 12th

Big things come in small packages

Can't solve a problem with the same mind that created it

April 14th

Revenge is like
drinking poison
and hoping it
will kill the
enemy

April 15th

True colors are shown when all isn't going one's way

April 16th

Externalizing negative emotions reflects how one feels about self

Love is truth at the heart of creation

April 18th

Relationships with other's reflects relationship with self

Transform inside out

April 20th

Neither beneath nor above anyone

Utter beauty in simplicity

April 22nd

Accomplish more by doing less

April 23rd

Evolve to the point of no return

April 24th

Give yourself a facelift with a smile

April 25th

The revolution starts within

April 26th

Be your quiet in a world full of thunder

Beautiful eyes cried the most tears

April 28th

Spiritual alchemy is greater than human thought

April 29th

Some of the prettiest smiles hide the darkest secrets

April 30th

Kindest hearts endured the most pain

May 1st

This too shall past

May 2nd

Wisdom is for the wise to teach the dumb

Enter action with boldness

May 4th

Master the art of timing

Recreate yourself

May 6th

Concentrate your forces

May 7th

Analyze the anal lies

May 8th

Stolen innocence stolen in a sense

Every problem has a soulution

May 10th

Act locally think globally

Someone's opinion doesn't have to be your reality

May 12th

If time flies, be the navigator

The harder you fall, the higher you bounce

Who's more foolish? The fool or the fool that follows?

The only silly question is the one never asked

May 16th

Your mind is exposed every time you speak

You are unique just like everyone else

May 18th

Never test the depths of something with both feet

Experience helps you recognize a mistake when repeated

May 20th

Build the new for the old to be obsolete

The only constant is change

May 22nd

Vision without execution is hallucination

Discover through intuition

May 24th

Our thoughts are tools we use to paint the canvas of our lives

Dip your brush into your own soul and paint your nature in those pictures

May 26th

Lose the fear of being wrong in order to truly be creative

Plan but let God take care of the details

May 28th

Everything articulated is plagiarized

Try again with a different approach

May 30th

Create your life don't be created by it

Imagination is the anticipation of attractions hoped for

June 1th

Who looks outside dreams but who looks inside awakes

June 1th

Who looks outside dreams but who looks inside awakes

The most responsive to change always survive

June 3rd

If you're not living on edge, you're taking up too much room

When everything is going your way, you're on the wrong path

June 5th

Growth is found among those who don't agree with you

Don't be in a hurry to swallow when chewing is pleasant

June 7th

The river may be wide but it can be crossed

2

Too much chatter leaves the mind empty

June 9th

Keep your dome light

Love is love when it affects both sides

June 11th

Even when thin, the thread of transparency never snaps

Face the bees in pursuit of honey

June 13th

Better to do it right than do it big

Kindness vanishes when not acknowledged on both ends

June 15th

What don't kill you build you

Don't cry if you let the same dog bite you twice

June 17th

If you're lazy, you deserve an empty stomach

Stolen food never suffices hunger pains

June 19th

Delay is the best remedy for anger

When light comes, darkness removes itself

June 21st

Things are
harder only
when you choose
to go uphill

June 22nd

The horizon will not disappear as you run towards it

June 23rd

Love all, trust a little, and wrong no one

Be open to change but keep your values close

June 25th

Home is where you are innerstood not where you live

Patience is bitter but bears sweet fruit

June 27th

A tree that grows in the shade of another dies young

The heart rules without rules

June 29th

If a full moon loves you, kiss the stars

Touched by words yet moved by action

A gem can't be polished without friction

Great souls have wills but feeble souls only wish

July 3rd

The wise make decisions but fools follow opinions

July 4th

Heaven lent you a soul but Earth will guarantee you a grave

The thorn of a rose only injures those that threaten its blossom

Beauty is the wisdom of women but wisdom is the beauty of men

July 7th

Insanity is doing the same thing and expecting a different result

July 8th

Look for something until you find it and you won't lose your labor

July 9th

Tread softly and you'll go far

Hear and forget, see and retain yet do and innerstand

July 11th

Sacrificing conscience for ambition is like burning a picture for ashes

Small ills shows
that we trip on
stones not
mountains

More important to know where you're going than get there quickly

A lie has speed but the truth has endurance

July 15th

Easy to dodge responsibilities but not the consequences

Dismiss what offends your soul

When they judge, they reveal who they are

Character is tested when given power

July 19th

If you can't change a situation, change yourself

What your enemy uses to frighten you is what they're most scared of

The undeserving of it need love the most

Don't trim yourself to suit everyone, you'll whittle yourself away

July 23rd

You can stand tall without standing on someone

Be a victor without victims

July 25th

Everyone is nobody to somebody so humble yourself

Great minds discuss ideas but small minds discuss people

July 27th

When you follow you fall low to another...be your own leader

Life's too short to nurse animosity

July 29th

There's enough for everyone's need not greed

Forgiveness enlarges the future

July 31st

If criticism isn't just, continue what you were doing

We can decide what happens in us not to us

August 2nd

Experience is how you interpret what happens to you

Go to extremes to find balance

August 4th

What starts in wrath ends in disdain

Slow to take, quick to give

August 6th

If you regret what past, you lose now and risk later

If your mouth is sharp, you might cut your lips

August 8th

Best mattress to sleep on is covered in peace

August 9th

Conserve your energy

August 10th

Nothing ventured, nothing gained

Perseverance is better than defeat

August 12th

You're only taken for granted when you allow it

Different strokes for different folks

August 14th

You're twice bound when your chains feel comfortable

A wombman is more than her breasts: goats have them too

August 16th

Too much excitement is an invitation to danger

When times are hardest, the brightest is near

August 18th

A phobia's power lies in our fear in it

Break down the boxes of society

August 20th

Live within your means

Don't reveal too much too soon

August 22nd

Send not a child on errands for an adult

Preserve the branch you climbed

August 24th

You lose when you fear risk

You know what
you've been
through but
what's to come is
always a mystery

August 26th

Can't teach an old dog new tricks

August 27th

You bury opportunities when you kill time

You bury opportunities when you kill time

August 28th

Charity always came from the heart not money

The want of a thing is sometimes more than it's worth

August 30th

Every head must do its own thinking

Why point 1 finger at someone when 3 get pointed back at you?

September 1st

The mind is a fire to be kindled

Lose sight of the shore than you can cross the ocean

September 3rd

Choices reveal who you are more than your abilities

You get exactly what you are willing to settle for

September 5th

You were born an original, don't die a counterfeit

September 6th

The pen that writes your life must be held by you

253

September 7th

Out of convolution, find tranquility

From dissonance, find peace

September 9th

In the midst of tribulation lies a way out

We might be a product of our environment but we're responsible for who we become

September 11th

We all live under the sun but have different horizons

Hands that serve are holier than lips that pray

September 13th

Finding out why you were born is most important

Live out your dreams not your fears

September 15th

There is a time to let things happen and when to make them happen

Time is socially constructed. What are you building on it?

September 17th

Wisdom knows the path, integrity walks it

Having no purpose is like a ship with no wheel

September 19th

Communion with God only comes through love

Soul's rainbow is a result of teardrops

September 21st

The hotter the battle the sweeter the victory

Give without remembering

September 23rd

Take without forgetting

Stir up gratitude and taste heaven

September 25th

Perceive the world adequately with a quiet mind

September 26th

Let it flow

September 27th

The more conscious you become, the more you realize how unconscious you were

Faith is the bird that feels the light and sings when it's still dark

September 29th

Bring your awareness to now and receive meditation

The best teachers tell you where to look but not what to see

October 1st

Plan for tomorrow but live for today

October 2nd

The lamps by many coming from one light source

October 3rd

What's not brought up in consciousness, comes by in fate

The life you lead is more important that the creed you profess

October 5th

Like a boomerang: the more stretched you are spiritually, the further you will go

When you pretend something is true, you become the lie

October 7th

Being defeated and giving up aren't the same

Keep money on your mind not your heart

October 9th

Your truest wealth is measured when you lose it all

Livity is measured by depth not length

October 11th

Ships are safe in the harbor but that's not what they are there for

The darkest hour only has 60 minutes

October 13th

We make a living by what we get but make a life in what we give

Your heart tells you what to do long before your mind can figure it out

October 15th

Help others while climbing but make sure you're closer to the top

Confront your problems and they will seem smaller than before

October 17th

Courage masters fear but isn't independent of it

October 18th

The art of living is sketched in growing with your troubles

October 19th

Those who try to pull you down prove you are beneath them

Never tear down a fence until you know why it was up there

If you get ahead too far from the army, you may be mistaken for the enemy

Love can make a summer fly or a night feel like a lifetime

October 23rd

We often change and forget to tell each other

Have something to say as opposed to just saying something

October 25th

People who matter recognize who you are

October 26th

The gift of listening brings the gift of healing

October 27th

Speak on experience or observation and question the rest

October 28th

Weeping may endure for the night but joy comes in the morning

October 29th

Love is touching souls

What goes up must come down

October 31ˢᵗ

Decisions shape the quality of your life

November 1st

Price of excellence is discipline

November 2nd

Cost of mediocrity is disappointment

See sunshine where others see shadows

November 4th

See opportunities where others see obstacles

If your ship doesn't come in, swim out to it

November 6th

Compromise to make the other feel like they got the bigger piece of the cake

November 7th

We can't control the wind but we can adjust the sail

November 8th

Weather the storm and dance in the rain

Do something you've never done to get something you never had

November 10th

A calm ocean never made a skilled surfer

Great leaders value emulation

November 12th

Trial and error is better than being doomed for not trying at all

A small leak can sink a big ship

November 14th

Can't shake hands with a clenched fist

Change something you do daily and you can change your life

November 16th

If you settle for less than you deserve, you get less than what you settled for

The cave you most fear to enter contains the greatest treasure

November 18th

See your fear as hurdles

Each day comes with a new gift and we are required to untie the ribbons

November 20th

Bask while the sun is shining

Don't get out picked in your own field

November 22nd

Don't let your mouth carry you from where your foot can't bring you from

Chase away someone with reason and they will not return

November 24th

The horse can carry you to the battlefield but you must fight

Alone the young run fast, with the elder slow, together very far

November 26th

Small trickles of water make a flood

Talking about fire doesn't boil the pot

November 28th

Running towards good fortune entails running away from peace

Don't set sail on someone else's star

November 30th

Start a journey in honesty and you'll find your way

December 1st

Long road draws sweat but the short road draws blood

December 2nd

Give good to who it is due

It's not what they say but what you answer to

December 4th

Today belongs to those who prepare for tomorrow

December 5th

Don't par with evildoers: you'll get tainted

December 6th

Let your mind acknowledge what your heart discerns

Don't throw pearls to swine

December 8th

Prodigal son

Don't worship the blessing, be thankful for the source

December 10th

Diligent hands bring forth wealth

Walk in integrity and feel secure

December 12th

Acknowledge constructive criticism to avoid going astray

Bite your tongue if necessary

December 14th

Accurate weights should weigh in the balance, not dishonest scales

If the word is a stage, know when to play your part

December 16th

If all is possible, 10 out 9 can be achieved

The course of true love doesn't ever run smooth

December 18th

Good intentions pave the road to hell

December 19th

Divided we stand, united we fall

December 20th

Eye am the cause, see the effect?

Don't care too much: you'll hurt yourself

December 22nd

Pray together, stay together

December 23rd

Knowing you know nothing makes you wise

December 24th

Expectation is the root to all heartache

Be merry as much as possible

December 26th

Be a big bargain if you're going to gamble in this life

December 27th

Smell the roses

December 28th

Be the change you want to see in the world

All good things come to an end so enjoy them while they last

December 30th

Twin soul mate > one night bait

December 31st

Create your own reality

Available on Amazon!

SCATTERED THOUGHTS: A STREAM OF CONSCIOUSNESS

FELICIA GUY-LYNCH

Available on iTunes!

Notes

_____

_____

_____

_____

_____

_____

_____

_____

_____

_____

_____

_____

_____

_____

_____

_____

_____

_____

_____

_____

_____

_____

Made in the USA
Charleston, SC
20 March 2013